Struik Pocket Guides for Southern Africa

Snakes

Rod Patterson
DIRECTOR, TRANSVAAL SNAKE PARK

ILLUSTRATED BY
Penny Meakin

STRUIK

Contents

Introduction 3
Field notes and species illustrations 4
Predation chart 49
Legislation and conservation 50
Locomotion 51
Scalation 51
Dentition 53
Reproduction 54
Husbandry 56
Snake bite treatment 58
Glossary 60
Suggested further reading 61
Index 63

Acknowledgements

Most of the illustrations in this guide were drawn from snakes housed in the Transvaal Snake Park reptile collection. However, in certain instances we had to call upon the resources of others.

We thus gratefully acknowledge the advice, the loan of preserved material and the photographs provided by Wulf Haacke of the Transvaal Museum. We thank too Richard Boycott, Curator of the Transvaal Snake Park, who made photographs available to us, and his assistant Dave Morgan who 'arranged' the specimens for the illustrator's convenience. We are also grateful to John Carlyon, Austin Stevens and Chris Stuart for providing photographs.

The illustrator wishes to thank her parents for their constant support.

Finally, we are indebted to Colleen Patterson who deciphered the author's handwriting and typed the manuscript – without her help and efficiency this guide would not have materialized.

ROD PATTERSON
PENNY MEAKIN
AUGUST 1986

Introduction

In southern Africa, that is, south of a line drawn from the Kunene River in the west to the Zambezi in the east, 160 species and subspecies of snakes are known to occur. These have managed to colonize almost every type of ecological niche on the subcontinent, and range from the snow-clad Drakensberg to the wind-blown Namib, from Table Mountain through the arid Karoo, and frost-ridden highveld to the Okavango swamps. Only the mountain peaks above the snowline in Lesotho tend to be devoid of snakes.

Snakes are 'cold-blooded' or, more correctly, ectothermic, which means that they regulate their body temperature mainly by means of external sources of heat. Cold greatly reduces the metabolic rate in snakes and consequently a greater number of species is found in tropical and subtropical areas than in the temperate zones and at the poles.

It is generally accepted that snakes evolved from some lizard-like ancestor; thus they are the most 'modern' group of reptiles. Their body skeletons are fragile and as a result the fossil record is quite sparse but they certainly have existed in their serpent form since the Cretaceous period some 100 million years ago.

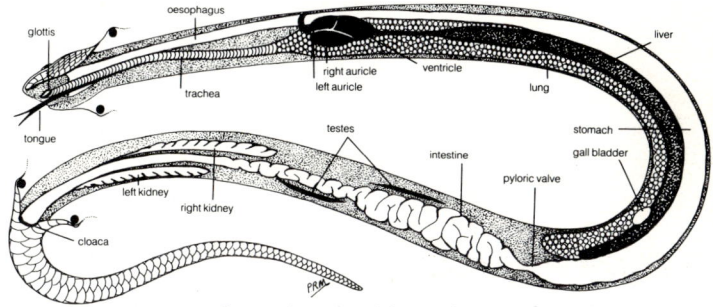

Internal organs of the snake

The loss of limbs and general attenuation of the body has resulted in a 'rearrangement' of some of the internal organs. Most snakes possess only a single functional lung, the right, which stretches at least a third of the body length. The left lung is sometimes absent; if it is present then it is usually small or rudimentary. The heart is situated between a sixth and a third of the way down the body. The liver, which is positioned behind the heart, is lengthened and extends from a third to half way down the body. The kidneys are also elongated and do not lie adjacent to each other, the right always being more anterior than the left.

The snake has no eyelids, the eye being covered by a translucent lens-cap which is periodically shed together with the external layer of skin. As herpetologist Clifford Pope so aptly writes: 'It manages to sleep with the eyes open, like some human beings'. It also has no external ear openings, so is deaf to airborne sound, although it does detect vibration through the substrate on which it is lying.

The forked tongue is one of the most familiar features of a snake. Being deaf and not blessed with very good eyesight (some species are almost blind), the snake's tongue is arguably its most important organ. The flickering tips pick up scent particles in the air which, when retracted into the mouth, are 'brushed' over two openings in the palate. These openings lead, via a duct along which the scent particles are wafted, to the organs of Jacobson where the particles are 'smelt' or 'tasted' by the sensory lining. Thus a snake is able to follow the 'scent trail' of a frog or mouse, a mate or even its own odour, enabling it to return with unerring accuracy to its particular hole or retreat among a jumble of foliage or rocks.

Of the 160 species and subspecies occurring in southern Africa, 53 have been selected for this pocket guide. Most of them are fairly common in their particular habitats. Some, such as the Quill-snouted snakes, have a wide distribution but are seldom seen because of their fossorial existence.

It is possible that you will at some time encounter a snake which cannot be identified from the following pages. Take either a clear colour photograph or the specimen itself to your local museum, zoo or reptile park and the experts there should be able to identify it for you.

It is hoped that this book will engender an interest in these 'lower' vertebrates which, after all, have existed on this planet for far longer than man.

Legends

The **distribution maps** show the areas in which each species is likely to occur. It is, however, possible that they may extend beyond these limits

 indicates those snakes which are potentially lethal to man

Field notes and species illustrations

Bibron's Blind Snake
Typhlops bibronii □ 30-40 cm

One of seven species of Blind Snake in southern Africa. Well adapted to a fossorial existence, the body is covered with fine, shiny scales. The tiny eyes appear as black dots below the head shields and the crescent-shaped mouth is situated on the underside of the head. The stubby tail ends in a short spike.

It feeds on insects, especially termite larvae which it hunts underground. Normally only seen above ground after heavy rains when flooding forces it to the surface, or when it is accidentally unearthed.

This harmless snake lays 5-12 eggs which hatch within a week. ☐ **Bibron se Erdslang.**

Schlegel's Blind Snake
Typhlops schlegelii subsp. ☐ 60-90 cm

There are three subspecies which are confined to the warmer northern parts of southern Africa. Both striped and mottled colour phases occur. Habits are similar to Bibron's Blind Snake. Although these are the largest of the Blind Snakes, big specimens are rarely seen because they apparently live at greater depths in the soil. Lays 12-60 eggs in early summer which hatch some 4-6 weeks later. ☐ **Reuse Erdslang.**

Peters' Worm or Thread Snake
Leptotyphlops scutifrons scutifrons □ 17-27 cm

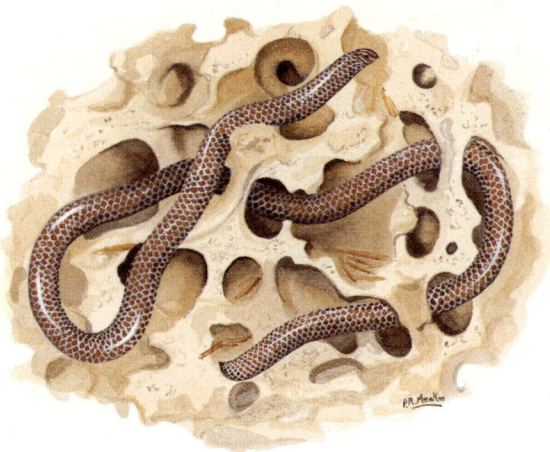

Nine species of Worm Snake occur in southern Africa, Peters' being by far the most common. Like the Blind Snakes it has vestigial eyes and a polished cylindrical body, but is far smaller and much more slender, hence its common name of 'thread snake'.

Normally found in termitaria or under leaf litter and amongst decomposing vegetable matter such as rotten logs, where it hunts tiny insects. Lays 3-6 eggs at a time. □ **Glansende Erdslangetjie.**

Southern African Python or Rock Python
Python sebae natalensis □ 3-6 m

The largest snake in southern Africa. Found in bushveld country, usually close to permanent water in which it enjoys lying for lengthy periods.

Juveniles feed on small rodents, progressing to larger prey such as rock hyrax, pheasant and guinea fowl. Adults take smaller forms of antelope, for example steenbuck, and large pythons can capture kudu calves and impala. Pythons have 'heat receptors' on their lips to detect the warmth of their prey, thus enabling them to strike accurately even in the dark. The sharp, recurved teeth bite into the prey and immediately thereafter the snake throws a number of coils around it. At each exhalation of the animal the pressure of the coils is increased until the animal dies from suffocation. No bones are crushed or intentionally broken. Once the heartbeat of the prey ceases, the python relaxes its coils and with its flickering tongue investigates the corpse, and then swallows it head first. After a large meal a python can remain without food for 3-6 months.

Mating occurs late July through August. Females lay 15-100 eggs per clutch from October to December. Unlike most other species which abandon their eggs, throughout the 80-100 day incubation period the female python remains coiled around her clutch to protect it and to increase the temperature, only leaving the eggs to drink. She does not feed during this time. Approximately 24 hours before they hatch the mother abandons the clutch. Hatchlings measure 50-60 cm. □ **Gewone Luislang.**

Brown Water-snake
Lycodonomorphus rufulus □ 60-90 cm

Always found in the vicinity of permanent water such as marshes, vleis, ponds and streams. Mostly nocturnal, it may be seen during rainy evenings as it hunts for frogs, which form a large part of its diet. It is an excellent swimmer and frequently captures fish underwater which it then takes to the shore and eats. In addition fledgelings, particularly weavers, are taken from

Brown Water-snake (cont.)

their nests. This inoffensive constrictor is often kept in captivity as a pet. In midsummer lays 6-10 eggs which hatch after 45-60 days. Hatchlings are 15-20 cm long. □ **Bruin Waterslang.**

Aurora Snake
Lamprophis aurora □ 60-90 cm

One of southern Africa's prettiest snakes, its yellow-orange vertebral stripe is quite distinctive. This nocturnal constrictor is frequently found near human habitation and, as a result of its quiet and inoffensive disposition, it is frequently kept in captivity as a pet. However, this practice, as well as farming operations and urban development, are leading to the numbers of this species being depleted.

Juveniles feed mainly on lizards whereas adults prey almost exclusively on small rodents. Lays 5-12 eggs during early summer and hatching occurs in December/January. Juveniles closely resemble the Striped Harlequin Snake (p. 21). ☐ **Aurora Nagslang.**

Brown House-snake
Lamprophis fuliginosus ☐ 80-120 cm

Undoubtedly the most common harmless snake in southern Africa. This nocturnal constrictor is frequently found near human habitation (hence its common name), where it hunts mice and rats. Juveniles include lizards in their diet.

Depending upon distribution the body colour may vary from light to dark brown; however, the two cream-coloured lines along the sides of the head are usually distinctive features.

Quite aggressive when initially cornered or molested the House-snake can become very tame and, under suitable conditions, will readily reproduce in captivity. Lays 6-25 eggs during November/December which hatch 50-80 days later. ☐ **Bruin Huisslang.**

Cape Wolf Snake
Lycophidion capense capense □ 40-60 cm

The Cape Wolf Snake is the most widely distributed of the four species of Wolf Snake in southern Africa. Nocturnal, it preys on small lizards (skinks) which it bites and then constricts. The teeth are relatively long and recurved (hence its common name), an adaptation to enable it to grasp its smooth-scaled prey.

During winter it is frequently found hibernating in termitaria together with the Egg-eater, House-snake and Black-headed Snake.

Lays 6-8 eggs during summer. □ **Kaapse Wolfslang.**

Common Slug-eater
Duberria lutrix lutrix □ 20-40 cm

A relatively small, inoffensive snake which feeds on slugs and snails and hence is of value to the gardener. Inhabits moist situations, such as rock piles, pond margins and beneath logs, where its prey abounds. Snails are bitten and then 'pulled' out of their shells, which frequently results in epic struggles.

When alarmed, this species rolls itself up like a coiled spring or roll of tobacco, resulting in its Afrikaans colloquial name of 'tabakrolletjie'.

Gives birth to 6-12 young during summer. Neonates are 6-10 cm in length.
☐ **Gewone Slakvreter.**

Cape File Snake
Mehelya capensis capensis ☐ 100-140 cm

By no means common, this inoffensive, nocturnal species inhabits warm bushveld areas. The vertebral line of white scales is distinctive. The keeled dorsal scales do not overlap and thus the purplish interstitial skin is clearly visible. In cross section the body is almost triangular and this, together with its rough scales, has given rise to the species' common name.

Diet consists mainly of other snakes, with a preference for Brown House-snakes, although species such as Cobras, Mole Snakes and Water Snakes are also taken. Prey is bitten at any point along the body. The File Snake manoeuvres the victim until the head is reached, and then swallows it without further ado. During this process the prey frequently coils around its attacker: venomous snakes may even bite the File Snake, but with no effect as it displays an immunity to other snake venoms. Occasionally toads and small rodents are also eaten.

Although extremely docile, it is held in awe by most African tribes and is considered by them to be highly venomous.

Lays 5-9 eggs during summer. ☐ **Kaapse Vylslang.**

Mole Snake
Pseudaspis cana □ 1-2 m

Adult

Colour is extremely variable. In the southern part of its range it is normally ebony, but farther north it becomes paler and is found in hues of grey, brown, red-brown, biscuit and yellow. Juveniles are yellow-brown with a series of dark brown or black blotches. Scales are smooth and shiny. The head is roundly pointed and flows into the muscular body.

A powerful constrictor, it is well adapted to pushing through loose soil and down rodent holes after its prey of moles, rats, gerbils and the like. It is, unfortunately, an irascible species, hissing and biting viciously when molested. This behaviour, together with its size, gives the impression that it is a dangerous species and frequently results in its unnecessary slaughter.

Unlike the males of other species where a form of combat 'dance' takes place, Mole Snakes actively fight each other, biting and inflicting deep parallel gashes across the body, often to the extent that bones are exposed.

Juvenile

Black colour morph

Biscuit colour morph

Because of its economic worth to the farmer, this species was one of the first snakes to be protected by law in the Cape. This also saved it from exploitation by the 'pet trade' since despite its initial aggressiveness it soon settles down in captivity.

Mating normally occurs during October and 30-50 (exceptionally 95) young are born during March/April. Neonates measure about 20 cm in length. □ **Molslang.**

Common Egg-eater
Dasypeltis scabra □ 40-90 cm

Resembles the Common Night Adder (p. 41), but is more slender and the V-shaped marking begins at the nape of the neck and not on top of the head as in the Night Adder.

As a result of its specialized diet of birds' eggs, the mouth is almost toothless. The egg is swallowed whole and 'cracked' in the throat region by

Common Egg-eater (cont.)

Head showing V-shaped marking

Egg being swallowed

Regurgitated shell

muscular contractions, the contents are swallowed and the crushed shell is regurgitated.

Although completely harmless, when threatened this species throws its body into a series of coils which causes the keeled lateral scales to rub together and emit an abrasive sound similar to that of scouring sandpaper. This is accompanied by repeated striking with the mouth agape, exposing the dark interior.

Lays 6-18 eggs in summer/autumn which take 3-4 months to hatch.
□ **Gewone Eiervreter.**

Cape Many-spotted or Reed Snake
Amplorhinus multimaculatus □ 50 cm

In the Cape, this species frequents damp localities such as vleis and marshes, but elsewhere it usually occurs in montane grassland. Two colour morphs exist: those in the Cape Peninsula and eastern Zimbabwe appear spotted whereas those from Natal and the Transvaal have a more uniform olive coloration.

Diet mainly consists of frogs although small rodents are occasionally taken. Initially aggressive, coiling and striking quite vigorously, the mouth and teeth of this snake are too small to harm humans.

Gives birth to four or five young, 12-20 cm long. ☐ **Kaapse Rietslang.**

Rufous Beaked Snake
Rhamphiophis oxyrhynchus rostratus ☐ 1-1,3 m

A diurnal bushveld species. When moving, the head, which has a distinctly hooked snout, jerks from side to side.

Although mildly venomous, this inoffensive snake rarely attempts to bite. Because of its small mouth, the diet is restricted to smaller prey such as insects, as well as rodents, lizards, frogs and other snakes.

Usually lays 6-17 eggs during October. ☐ **Haakneusslang.**

Spotted Skaapsteker
Psammophylax rhombeatus rhombeatus

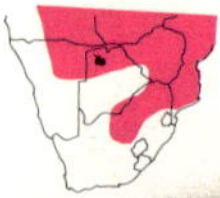

Striped Skaapsteker
Psammophylax tritaeniatus ☐ 75-100 cm

Spotted Skaapsteker

Striped Skaapsteker

Both species are found in open grasslands. They are diurnal and prey on lizards, frogs and small rodents which they hunt at speed. Although venomous (but with no human fatalities recorded), Skaapstekers will, after biting their prey, often coil around it.

The common name is misleading as these snakes are incapable of killing anything as large as a sheep. They are, however, frequently found in the vicinity of kraals, the walls of which provide them with cover as well as food in the form of rock-dwelling lizards.

They lay 6-30 eggs in summer. The Spotted Skaapsteker female remains with her clutch during the month-long incubation period. Hatchlings measure 16-20 cm in length. ☐ **Skaapsteker** ☐ **Gestreepte Skaapsteker.**

Cape Centipede-eater or Black-headed Snake
Aparallactus capensis □ 25-30 cm

The diminutive 'Blackhead' is a fossorial species found among grass roots and leaf litter. It often hibernates in disused termitaria, a fact abused by some collectors who smash open antheaps during winter and catch dozens of these inoffensive snakes. The species seldom survives in captivity.

It is occasionally seen at night, particularly after summer rains, when it searches for its staple food of centipedes. The venom is of no consequence to humans; in fact, the tiny teeth are incapable of piercing the skin.

Lays 2-4 eggs. □ **Swartkop-mierslang.**

Striped Quill-snouted Snake
Xenocalamus bicolor lineatus □ 40-58 cm

Four species of Quill-snouted Snake occur in southern Africa, all of which have elongated bodies, small heads and long, pointed snouts resembling the archaic quill pen. The Striped Quill-snout is nocturnal and fossorial,

Striped Quill-snouted Snake (cont.)

inhabiting deep sand. It eats various species of burrowing, limbless reptiles.
Lays 2-4 elongated eggs in midsummer which hatch in early March.
☐ **Spitsneus-grondslang.**

Grass and Sand Snakes
Psammophis spp. ☐ 30-120 cm

Nine species occur in southern Africa. The various forms are widely
distributed in habitats that vary from the Namib desert and karroid scrub to
bushveld, highveld savanna and montane grasslands. Most do not exceed
1 metre in length. The Olive Grass Snake *P. phillipsii* which is a uniform

Olive Grass Snake *P. phillipsii*. The longest and most robust of the Grass
Snakes, a large specimen could be mistaken for a young Black Mamba.

Short-snouted Sand Snake *P. sibilans brevirostris*. A lateral view of the body scales showing the typical striped pattern of this group.

Stripe-bellied or Yellow-bellied Sand Snake *P. subtaeniatus subtaeniatus*. A ventral view showing the brightly coloured belly of this species.

Cross-marked Grass Snake *P. crucifer*. So named because of the markings on the top of the head, it rarely exceeds 60 cm in length.

Forked-marked Sand Snake *P. leightoni trinasalis*. So called because of its head markings, this species can attain 1 m in length.

yellowish olive-brown colour, may attain 1,7 metres in length and is the largest of the group.

All the other forms have some degree of striped patterning with parallel bands running from head to tail. Their mild venom is of no consequence to humans; in fact, there is no striped snake in South Africa which is dangerous to man.

Although the larger species may become quite robust, all are nevertheless slender, extremely agile and swift snakes, attributes which enable them to actively hunt for their prey which to a large extent consists of various species of lizards, particularly skinks and agamas. Also included in their diet are other snakes (a captured 140 cm Olive Grass Snake is on record as having disgorged a 67 cm Black Mamba), small rodents and frogs.

As a result of their wide distribution, fairly common occurrence and diurnal behaviour, Sand Snakes in turn provide a valuable source of food to other predators, particularly birds of prey such as the Snake Eagles *Circaetus* spp. Those snakes which survive this predation often have the ends of their tails missing.

Depending on the species, clutches range from 4-20 eggs which are laid during the summer months.☐ **Sand-** en **Sweepslange.**

Southern or Sundevall's Shovel-snout
Prosymna sundevallii sundevallii □ 25 cm

Six species of Shovel-snout occur in southern Africa, all of them characterized by the enlarged rostral shield with horizontal cutting edge. In some species, such as Sundevall's Shovel-snout, the cutting edge is slightly upturned.

Although fairly common within its range, this little snake is not often encountered because of its fossorial existence: normally it is found in old termitaria or under flat slabs of rock. When disturbed it curls and uncurls its body in a vigorous and erratic fashion in an attempt to deter the aggressor. It is, however, harmless to man.

Diet consists of reptile eggs – either the soft-shelled eggs of snakes and some lizards, or hard-shelled gecko eggs.

Relatively small clutches of eggs are laid, 3-4 being the norm.
□ Graafneusslang.

Spotted Harlequin Snake
Homoroselaps lacteus □ 30-40 cm

Coloration is variable, although in most the head is black with individual scales dotted yellow or orange. Some specimens are yellowish white above with 30-50 black crossbands on the body, while others are black with irregularly spaced yellowish white crossbands interspersed with red and yellow flecks on the sides. There is also a striped colour phase.

This brightly coloured fossorial snake is frequently found in old termitaria or under slabs of rock resting on sandy soil. The diet consists of small Worm and Blind snakes as well as burrowing skinks. In the unlikely event of this inoffensive snake biting a human, its venom would have little effect.

Lays as many as six eggs in midsummer. ☐ **Kousbandslangetjie, Kousbandjie.**

Striped Harlequin Snake
Homoroselaps dorsalis ☐ 30 cm

More limited in distribution than the previous species, the Striped Harlequin Snake with its distinctive yellow stripe running from head to tail may be confused with the striped colour phase of the Spotted Harlequin Snake or possibly a young Aurora Snake (pp. 8-9).

Little is known about the habits of this innocuous snake, although they are probably similar to those of the Spotted Harlequin Snake. ☐ **Kousbandjie.**

Southern or Bibron's Stiletto Snake
Atractaspis bibronii □ 30-45 cm

Known for many years as the 'Mole Viper' or 'Burrowing Adder', it has been demonstrated that this snake is not an adder but is more closely related to fossorial species such as the Black-headed Snake (page 17). Superficially, although the Stiletto Snake resembles the harmless Wolf Snake (page 10) in colour and appearance, it has no distinct neck and has a sharp spike on its tail tip.

It is found in disused termitaria and under rocks and logs, but can be seen above ground on warm nights, particularly after heavy summer rains. Prey consists of other reptiles such as the Blind Snakes, burrowing lizards and small rodents.

In humans, the venom causes intense local pain which progresses to glands in the vicinity of the bite, followed by localized swelling. Partial to severe necrosis can occur days after the bite, but no fatalities have been recorded. Polyvalent antivenom is not effective and should not be used: treatment should be symptomatic.

As many as six elongated eggs are laid during summer. □ **Sypikslang.**

Green Water-snake or South-eastern Green Snake
Philothamnus hoplogaster □ 60 cm

Five species of Green or 'Bush' Snake occur in southern Africa. They may be mistaken for young Green Mambas (page 39) but Green Snakes have a proportionately larger eye than Mambas, and they have different distribution ranges.

The Green Snake is an agile, diurnal species normally found in the vicinity of streams and vleis, where reedbeds occur and trees overhang water. It

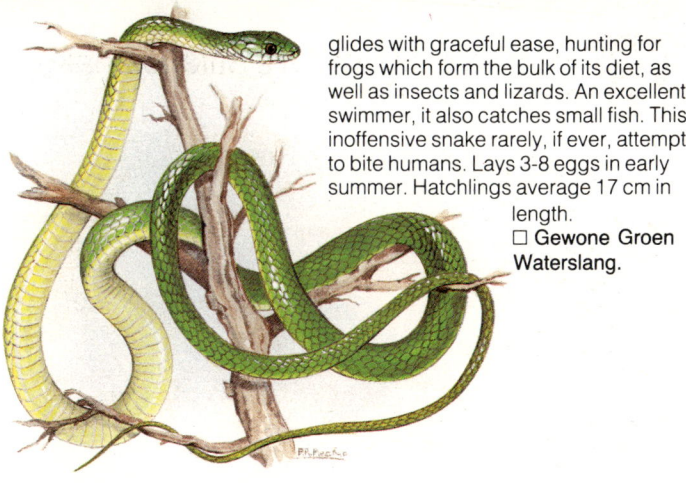

glides with graceful ease, hunting for frogs which form the bulk of its diet, as well as insects and lizards. An excellent swimmer, it also catches small fish. This inoffensive snake rarely, if ever, attempts to bite humans. Lays 3-8 eggs in early summer. Hatchlings average 17 cm in length.
☐ Gewone Groen Waterslang.

Spotted Bush Snake

Philothamnus semivariegatus semivariegatus ☐ 1 m

The Spotted Bush Snake has a far wider distribution than the Green Snake and is not as dependent on permanent water. Mainly arboreal, it also frequents rocky outcrops, particularly those where its prey of geckos and other rock-dwelling lizards live.

When threatened, this normally timid species inflates its throat in a similar fashion to the highly venomous Boomslang (page 26) and strikes out quite viciously. However, all *Philothamnus* species are harmless.

Lays 4-12 elongated eggs during summer.

☐ Gespikkelde Bosslang.

Herald Snake or Red-lipped Snake
Crotaphopeltis hotamboeia □ 50-100 cm

Widespread throughout southern Africa except in the arid western areas. Frequently found near human habitation in the vicinity of damp man-made structures such as fish ponds, dams and golf courses, as well as natural vleis and river banks. Nocturnal, its diet consists mainly of frogs and toads.

Although the red 'lips' are quite distinctive, occasional specimens have yellow, white or black markings along the upper jaw. When molested the snake flattens its head in viper-like fashion and displays the red flashes along its jaw line. However, its venom is so mild that it would not harm a cat or dog and certainly is of no consequence to humans, even small children.

It lays 6-30 eggs in spring to early summer. Incubation takes 40-90 days.

Hatching normally occurs when prey in the form of newly metamorphosed frogs is in abundance. Hatchlings (8-19 cm) resemble the adults but have a fine sprinkling of white dots over the olive body colour. ☐ **Rooilip-slang.**

Eastern Tiger Snake
Telescopus semiannulatus semiannulatus
40-70 cm, occasionally 100 cm

The strikingly coloured Tiger Snake has bulbous eyes and a flattened head distinct from its neck and slender body. Two other forms, namely *T. beetzii* and *T. s. polystictus* occur in the drier western half of southern Africa. It is closely related to the Herald Snake (page 24).

This nocturnal species is chiefly terrestrial but has been collected under exfoliating bark, metres from the ground, as well as in rock cracks while hunting for its prey which consists mainly of geckos and other small lizards. It is also partial to smaller types of nestling birds, particularly finches.

Always an irritable species, even after years in captivity, it will bite with the least provocation, normally chewing at the victim in order to imbed its fangs which are situated towards the rear of the mouth. As with the Herald Snake, the venom is mild and of minor consequence to humans, causing little more than local irritation.

It lays 6-17 eggs during the summer months. In captivity this species has been known to produce two fertile clutches during the same season – in early and midsummer. ☐ **Gewone Tierslang.**

Boomslang or Tree Snake
Dispholidus typus typus ☐ 1-1,5 m

The Boomslang is widely distributed throughout southern Africa, appearing in a number of different colour morphs depending on age, gender and locality. Colours range from a flecked grey, through brown, almost black, black and yellow to green. The males are usually more brightly coloured than the females. The diagnostic feature of the Boomslang, irrespective of colour, is the eye, which is the largest of all African snakes'. The rounded head is distinct from the moderately slender body and the dorsal scales are keeled.

As its name implies, this is an arboreal species and it preys largely on tree-dwelling lizards such as agamas, geckos and chameleons, as well as fledgelings and small rodents. However, the Boomslang may descend from its leafy domain and move over the ground or even swim across a stream in pursuit of its prey. Once the prey has been subdued, the snake will always retire to the safety of a shrub or tree before it swallows its victim.

Because of its docile temperament it was long thought to be a 'harmless' snake; however, under extreme provocation it inflates its throat and strikes out with its mouth wide agape. This allows the grooved fangs, which are situated towards the rear of the upper jaw, to come into contact with the flesh of its victim.

In humans, the venom is potently haemotoxic, causing extensive haemorrhaging of the mucous linings of the body. As internal bleeding

Irate Boomslang inflating its throat

All juvenile Boomslang have iridescent green eyes

Brown colour morph

Green colour morph

continues, large areas of the body will turn blue as a result of numerous clots beneath the skin and the kidneys can suffer irreparable damage. Death may occur some 3-5 days after the bite.

Fortunately, serious bites are extremely rare and most, in fact, are inflicted on snake handlers who actively expose themselves to the risk of envenomation by this normally shy and elusive snake. A limited supply of Boomslang-specific antivenom is available from the SAIMR on request by a doctor treating an identified bite.

Lays 10-25 eggs during spring which hatch some 70-100 days later.
☐ **Boomslang.**

Vine, Twig or Bird Snake
Thelotornis capensis subspp. ☐ 1-1,5 m

Three subspecies are recognized in southern Africa, namely *T. c. mossambicanus*, *T. c. oatesii* and *T. c. capensis* which differ mainly in head markings.

The lance-shaped head and the grey, bark-like coloration of the slender body make this arboreal snake one of the most effectively camouflaged species in Africa. It frequently protrudes the anterior third of its body from a branch and remains in this position for minutes on end. The disguise is maintained even during a breeze when the snake will sway in unison with the surrounding foliage.

Vine, Twig or Bird Snake (cont.)

Twig Snake in defensive display with throat inflated and tongue extended

A horizontal pupil and an indentation running from eye to snout give the Twig Snake excellent binocular vision and enable it to discern stationary prey which it stalks in an uncanny manner. Lying along a branch, the Twig Snake moves forward almost imperceptibly, creating the impression that the end of the branch is growing by the second. Once within striking distance of its prey, the snake lunges forward and grabs it by the nape. The jaws work vigorously to embed the back fangs into the victim and, often, while the snake is hanging head downwards, the prey is literally swallowed 'upwards'.

Arboreal lizards form the bulk of its diet, but fledgelings, frogs, small mammals and other snakes are also taken. When molested the Twig Snake, like the Boomslang, inflates the throat region in a defensive display, simultaneously flickering its black-tipped, bright orange tongue.

In humans, the venom, although producing haemotoxic effects similar to those of the Boomslang's, is not neutralized by Boomslang antivenom. As there is no antivenom available, victims are treated symptomatically, usually by means of whole blood infusions. Fortunately, fatal bites are extremely rare.

It lays 4-13 eggs in summer. □ **Voëlslang.**

Garter Snakes
Elapsoidea spp. ☐ 30-70 cm

Eight races of this genus occur in southern Africa. Typical of semi-fossorial species, their snouts are to some degree bluntly pointed, the scales are smooth and shiny and their bodies are relatively slender. Juveniles may be quite colourful, being dark brown to black with varying numbers of light pink, yellow, buff or brown crossbands which may persist faintly into adulthood.

Garter Snakes inhabit coastal plains, the Kalahari floodpan and highveld grasslands and have an extremely diverse diet which includes snakes, fossorial lizards, lizard eggs, frogs and small burrowing mammals. They are nocturnal and although they usually remain under logs, rock slabs and in termitaria or deep sand, they can be seen abroad on warm, wet evenings.

Little is known regarding the potency of their venom except that it causes localized pain; to date no fatalities have been recorded. Their placid demeanour notwithstanding, snakes in this genus should be accorded due respect as they are elapids (front-fanged snakes related to cobras and mambas), and are potentially dangerous.

Reproduction data is limited but it is known that some Garter Snakes lay up to 10 eggs. ☐ **Kousbandslang.**

Rinkhals
Hemachatus haemachatus □ 1-1,2 m

The juveniles are usually light grey above and black below with one to three distinct white neckbands, hence the common name 'rinkhals', meaning ringneck. As the snake matures the grey darkens to charcoal and the neckbands may fade, sometimes disappearing completely. A 'barred' colour form which has a black head and alternate yellowish cream and dark brown crossbands occurs in Natal. Dorsal scales are keeled and dull, ventrals are shiny.

This snake, which is endemic to southern Africa, is very common in certain areas and is often found close to human habitation. In the open veld it utilizes disused termitaria and rodent holes. Although it prefers toads, it also eats other snakes, as well as rodents, lizards, birds and their eggs.

As a defence when molested, the Rinkhals will raise the anterior portion of its body and spread a hood, thereafter lunging forward, repeatedly 'spitting' its venom at the aggressor. Venom is ejected through the fangs in two distinct jets which disperse into a spray – some of which enters the eyes of the attacker causing intense pain (see Snake bite treatment, page 58).

As a last resort when threatened, the snake will become completely limp, roll over the forepart of its body, hold its mouth agape and sham death. Close observation will invariably reveal that one eye is watching the attacker; touching or handling a 'dead' snake by the inexperienced usually results in a bite when the snake suddenly 'returns to life'. Polyvalent antivenom may be necessary in the treatment of a bite.

The Rinkhals produces 20-40 live young during midsummer. □ **Rinkhals.**

Coral Snake
Aspidelaps lubricus lubricus □ 40-60 cm

One of our most vivid snakes, it has alternate reddish orange bands and narrower black crossbars. The rostral or nose shield is quite pronounced in relation to the small head which flows into the smooth-scaled, robust body.

Inhabiting rock-strewn sandy areas it is a semi-fossorial species which usually emerges at night or after rain. It preys on small rodents, lizards and other snakes.

An easily irritated species, when disturbed it raises the anterior portion of its body and flattens its neck to spread a slender hood. This is accompanied by abrupt hissing and lunging at the antagonist. Its irate behaviour persists even after years in captivity. Little is known regarding the potency of its venom but the allied Western Coral Snake (*A. l. infuscatus*) is potentially dangerous.

The snake has been known to reproduce in captivity: small clutches of 2-5 eggs are laid during midsummer. □ **Koraalslang.**

Shield or Shield-nose Snake
Aspidelaps scutatus scutatus □ 50 cm

Three races of Shield Snake occur in the region and although they vary in colour, all have greatly enlarged nose shields. The squat head leads to a short thickset body, giving a viper-like appearance.

Mostly fossorial, it may be found under rock slabs, logs, or leaf litter in sandy areas, shoving its way below ground. It can be seen abroad on warm wet evenings, foraging for small rodents, toads, lizards and other snakes.

Its behaviour is typical of this group: rearing up and inflating its throat, it emits short sharp hisses while repeatedly lunging at its attacker. On occasion it will also sham death. Although information concerning its venom is limited, this species should be considered potentially dangerous.

Reproductive data is limited to the fact that it lays eggs.
□ Skildneusslang.

Egyptian, Banded or Bushveld Cobra
Naja haje annulifera □ 1-2,5 m

Most specimens have a dark brown or black band across the throat, a feature particularly conspicuous in juveniles. A banded phase occurs, in which the dark dorsal surface of the body is regularly interspaced with narrower, light yellow crossbands.

Typically a savanna species, it occurs from sea level to 1 500 metres. Disused termitaria, hollow logs or rocky outcrops are used as retreats and, provided it is not disturbed, the snake might remain in a particular area for years. It is largely nocturnal. Although it is partial to toads, lizards, rodents, birds and their eggs, and other snakes, all form part of its diet.

While not overtly aggressive, when molested the Egyptian Cobra will rear and spread an impressive hood. A two-metre specimen with the anterior 60 cm of its body raised and displaying a hood more than 12 cm wide, is an intimidating sight. Like most snakes, eyesight is quite limited and should the molester retreat, the cobra will advance in the rearing position to maintain visual contact. To the uninitiated this appears to be a form of attack. When the Egyptian Cobra bites its victim, it hangs on and chews tenaciously, embedding its short front fangs in the flesh and injecting a relatively large quantity of venom.

In humans, although the potent neurotoxic venom can cause death through respiratory failure, the polyvalent antivenom produced by the SAIMR is effective.

It lays up to 25 eggs. ☐ **Egiptiese Kobra, Bosveld Kapel.**

Banded colour morph

Cape Cobra
Naja nivea □ 1-2 m

The Cape Cobra, which is endemic to southern Africa, appears in a variety of colours ranging from black through mottled brown and yellow to a rich gold, but all have a glossy, almost plastic appearance. Juveniles are usually bright yellow with a distinctive black throat band.

The Cape Cobra is mainly found in the drier western half of the subcontinent but its distribution does extend down the wetter southern Cape coast and includes the western mountain slopes of Lesotho.

This agile, alert cobra is nocturnal in habit although it may be seen abroad during the day. Retreats in the form of disused rodent burrows, the abandoned nests of pied starlings excavated in the banks of dongas and dry river courses, as well as derelict houses and car wrecks are all utilized. Diet consists of rodents, toads, snakes (including its own kind), lizards, birds and their eggs. The Cape Cobra is preyed on by various species of mongoose.

As the Cape Cobra carries the most potent neurotoxin of all the African cobras, it is justifiably feared in those areas where it occurs. When antagonized it will rear, spread a hood and strike at the aggressor, advancing all the while. Even when 'backing off' it might suddenly swing round and strike should the antagonist get too close. The venom causes cardiac and respiratory failure in humans: prompt treatment with the polyvalent antivenom is essential.

Up to 20 eggs are laid in midsummer, hatchlings (30-40 cm) normally appearing in February/March. □ **Kaapse Geelslang, Kaapse Kobra.**

Forest Cobra
Naja melanoleuca ☐ 1,8-2,1 m

The largest of the southern African cobras, a specimen of 2,69 m has been recorded. Although it usually inhabits natural forests, it has adapted to areas where these have been replaced by tea or cane plantations.

The diet is typical of the cobras, consisting of frogs, toads, rodents and other snakes. It will also take to water in search of slow-moving fish such as catfish.

In defence it will rear and spread a long, slender hood which is much narrower than that of the other cobras. The neurotoxic venom is not as potent as that of the Cape Cobra, but nevertheless is lethal to humans. Treatment with the polyvalent antivenom is required.

Hardy and long-lived, many Forest Cobras have survived more than 15 years in captivity. Up to 26 eggs are laid in early summer, hatching in December/January. ☐ **Bontlipkobra, Boskobra.**

Western Barred Spitting Cobra
Naja nigricollis nigricincta □ 1-1,5 m

This inhabitant of central and northern Namibia has numerous irregular black crossbands over the body, a unique coloration amongst the African cobras: its Afrikaans name of 'Sebraslang' is most apt. In the north-western Cape this species is replaced by the Black Spitting Cobra (*N. nigricollis woodi*) which is jet black in colour.

The 'spitting' action is essentially a defence mechanism and the Barred Spitting Cobra normally rears before spitting its venom towards its attacker as a deterrent (see Moçambique Spitting Cobra, pp. 36-37). The venom is potently cytotoxic and a bite from this or an allied species causes severe tissue damage: a fact which in the past led to the erroneous belief that the Puff Adder (page 47) was the culprit.

As a result of their nocturnal habits and the frequency with which they are found near human habitation, the various races of Spitting Cobra probably account for a greater number of snake bites in Africa than the common Puff Adder. □ **Sebraslang.**

Moçambique Spitting Cobra or imFezi
Naja mossambica □ 1-1,5 m

A very common snake of the savanna and bushveld areas, often seen in the vicinity of kraals where the packed stone walls provide ideal retreats. It also utilizes old termitaria and disused rodent holes.

While juveniles are to a large extent diurnal, adults are usually abroad at night in search of their prey which consists mainly of toads. Other snakes, lizards, fledgelings and rodents are also taken when available.

Although it does rear and spread a hood in typical cobra fashion and spit from this position, this species is also capable of spitting from the horizontal position, such as from within the confines of a rock crack. Large, seemingly inexhaustible quantities of venom are directed towards the upper body of the attacker. On entering the eyes, the potent cytotoxic venom instantly creates an intense burning pain that causes both eyes and nose to run profusely. Unless promptly treated, the eyes can become ulcerated, resulting in partial to permanent blindness (see Snake bite treatment, page 58).

Besides spitting, the imFezi can and will bite, something which frequently happens when this snake enters rural dwellings where the inhabitants may be asleep on the floor and, in rolling over, inadvertently squash the snake which retaliates by biting. As with other Spitting Cobras, its venom causes localized pain and swelling followed by partial to severe necrosis around the bitten area. Depending on the severity of envenomation, tissue damage can occur along the bitten limb and even into the body.

It lays 10-22 eggs during the summer months. □ **Mosambiek Spoegkobra.**

Black Mamba
Dendroaspis polylepis
2,5-3,5 m

The Black Mamba is the longest venomous snake in Africa; worldwide, only the King Cobra (*Ophiophagus hannah*) attains a greater length. The Black Mamba is agile and sinuous, even in large specimens where the girth can be as thick as a man's wrist. The long coffin-shaped head and charcoal-coloured mouth lining are characteristic of this species, which is dull olive, gunmetal or leaden in colour with occasional darker mottlings.

An inhabitant of bushveld and tropical areas, it often holes up in disused termitaria, hollow tree trunks and rocky outcrops where it will stay indefinitely if undisturbed. Ritualistic combat behaviour (see Snouted Night-adder, p. 41) has been observed between male Black Mambas. Dassies are particularly favoured prey, but rodents and various game birds are also taken. Prey is struck once or twice and then left to succumb to the potent neurotoxin before being eaten.

It is a nervous and elusive species and as a result, fortunately, not many people come into contact with this snake. However, when confronted or cornered, a large, angry Black Mamba is an awesome sight. Swaying gently, the anterior third of its body is raised to almost human shoulder height. With its jaws agape, exposing the black mouth lining, and its narrow hood extended, the snake emits a low, hollow-sounding hiss. Even while on the move in this raised position, the Black Mamba can strike rapidly and repeatedly at its aggressor. The powerful nerve poison is injected into the victim in large quantities through the relatively long front fangs. The onset of erratic heartbeat and respiratory failure is rapid and only prompt administration of copious amounts of antivenom will ensure the victim's survival.

Some 6-14 eggs are laid in midsummer, hatching about 2½ months later. ☐ **Swart Mamba.**

Green Mamba
Dendroaspis angusticeps
1,5-3,3 m

This species superficially resembles the Black Mamba but does not attain the length of that species, and in coloration is a bright emerald green above, showing the occasional yellow-flecked scale. Juveniles tend to be a darker green. It has a limited distribution and does not occur in the Transvaal.

Shy and elusive, it does not display the aggressive temperament of its 'black' relative nor is its neurotoxic venom as potent, although it certainly is lethal. The arboreal Green Mamba blends well with its lush tropical environment and is thus rarely seen or encountered. Diet consists of small mammals and birds.

Up to 14 eggs are laid in early summer and hatching occurs in midsummer. ☐ **Groen Mamba.**

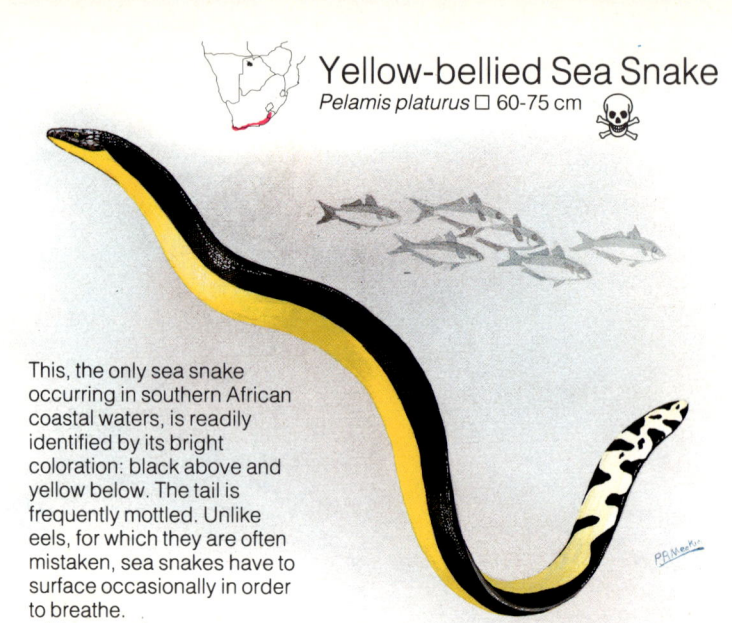

Yellow-bellied Sea Snake
Pelamis platurus □ 60-75 cm

This, the only sea snake occurring in southern African coastal waters, is readily identified by its bright coloration: black above and yellow below. The tail is frequently mottled. Unlike eels, for which they are often mistaken, sea snakes have to surface occasionally in order to breathe.

These snakes congregate among the marine debris which attracts the many species of small fish that constitute their diet.

As an adaptation to marine life the sea snake's body is laterally compressed, much like an oar blade on edge, and the snake is capable of swimming either forwards or backwards in short bursts of speed. Its dependence on ocean currents has certain disadvantages: storms may drive the snake into the surf area where it is powerless to escape the turbulence and will thus be stranded on the shore. As its flattened shape renders it incapable of progress on land, it merely falls over and consequently dies as it is unable to return to the sea. Also, ocean currents may propel sea snakes into the cooler waters around Cape Point and from there into the cold Benguela current where, inevitably, they will die.

Little is known regarding the potency of the Yellow-bellied Sea Snake's venom other than that it is a myotoxin, causing paralysis of the skeletal muscles.

This species gives birth in the ocean to 3-8 young, each about 25 cm in length. □ **Swart-en-geel Seeslang.**

Stranded Sea Snake

Common Night-adder
Causus rhombeatus □ 30-60 cm

Unlike most adders, the Common Night-adder does not have a pronounced head; it is only just distinct from the body. Although not always present, a characteristic feature is the dark brown V across the head.

Nocturnal, it preys on amphibians, particularly toads. It seldom strays from moist habitats. The fangs are quite short but are connected to extremely long venom glands. The relatively mild venom causes local swelling and glandular pain.

Up to 25 eggs are laid in early summer. □ **Nagadder.**

Snouted Night-adder
Causus defilippii □ 30-40 cm

The Snouted Night-adder is easily distinguished from the Common Night-adder by its upturned snout, shorter, stubbier body and more distinct markings. However, the habits of the two species are similar.

Male combat has been witnessed among both species of Night-adder. It takes the form of neck bumping and much jerky intertwining of the bodies. No biting is involved and once dominance has been established by one of the combatants, the vanquished male moves off. This 'combat dance' has frequently been incorrectly interpreted as mating behaviour.

Up to eight eggs are laid during summer. □ **Wipneus Nagadder.**

Horned Adder
Bitis caudalis □ 30-40 cm

Typically adder-shaped with a short stubby body, distinct neck and flat, triangular-shaped head. The basic colour is extremely variable, ranging from light grey through reddish orange to brown, with overlaying markings often pastel-shaded brown blotches with buff centres. Scales are keeled. The common name arises from the single, vertical 'hornlike' scale above each eye.

This species becomes progressively more colourful as its distribution radiates from the arid western half of the subcontinent to the east. The snakes also become more specific in dietary preference: whereas the desert-dwellers are extremely catholic in their diet, taking small lizards, snakes, birds and rodents, the eastern forms (especially when in captivity) tend to prefer lizards, particularly geckos, and very rarely take rodents. This snake is capable of 'sidewinding' but not to the degree displayed by the Peringuey's Adder (pp. 44-45).

It is an irascible species, hissing and lunging out repeatedly when molested. Although no human fatalities have been recorded the venom causes severe pain and necrosis around the bitten area. The use of antivenom is not indicated as the venom is not life-threatening, so a patient would be treated symptomatically.

From February to April the Horned Adder produces 4-19 young which average 13,5 cm in length. In neonates the hornlike structure above the eye apparently appears only as a diminutive 'bump' which develops with age.

□ Horingadder, Horingsmannetjie.

Western Many-horned Adder
Bitis cornuta cornuta □ 30-40 cm

Similar in appearance to the Horned Adder (page 42) although the coloration tends more to a grey or smoky blue. The identifying feature of this snake is the cluster of elongated, hornlike scales above each eye. This species is found from the western Cape north into Namibia, while an eastern form, *B.c. inornata*, extends into the south-eastern Cape.

In its habitat of arid areas, this species prefers rocky situations bordering on sand. Typical of the dwarf adders inhabiting the south-western corner of Africa and probably as a result of the harsh conditions under which it exists, the Many-horned Adder is an irascible species and strikes under the least provocation. The diet consists primarily of lizards, although rodents and snakes are also taken.

Few case histories of bites have been reported, but the venom caused severe pain in and local necrosis of the finger of a victim known to the writer.

It produces 8-20 young during late summer/early winter. The neonates possess a minute cluster of scales above each eye which gradually increase with age. □ **Veelhoringadder, Horingsmannetjie.**

Peringuey's Desert or Side-winding Adder
Bitis peringueyi □ 22-25 cm

This diminutive snake is confined to the Namib desert. It usually frequents the valleys between dunes where plants such as the shilling bush (*Zygophyllum stapfii*) grow. As sand collects in and around these shrubs it creates mounds which this species uses as retreats.

Peringuey's Adder has evolved a number of modifications to cope with its desert existence. One of these is the position of the eyes: they are situated on top of the head and not to the sides as in other snakes. By performing a series of lateral movements, the snake is able to 'sink' into the soft sand within seconds, leaving only its upward-facing eyes exposed above the surface. This sand-sinking action not only provides protection from the fierce heat on the surface, it is also an effective form of camouflage. Normally the snake positions the tip of its tail near its head and moves it either above or below the sand to act as a lure to dune-dwelling lizards which believe it to be an insect and thus come within the snake's striking distance.

As a further modification, Peringuey's Adder has a side-winding mode of progression which enables it to traverse the loose, wind-blown sand and even scale the 45° slipface of a dune. This 'rolling' over the surface also minimizes contact with the hot sand.

Movement from the retreat mounds to the hunting sites along the dune slipfaces depends upon seasonal variations: during the hot months activity

By performing a series of lateral movements, the Peringuey's Adder is able to 'sink' into the soft desert sand within seconds, leaving only its upward-facing eyes exposed above the surface

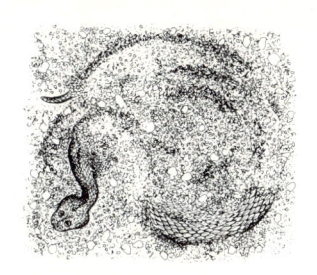

is mostly at night whereas in the cooler periods the snakes are abroad during the day.

Along the Namib coast, a heavy fog intermittently sweeps in over the desert and provides a source of moisture for the desert's inhabitants. On these occasions Peringuey's Adder surfaces and, by flattening its body, presents a larger area onto which the fine mist settles. The snake then moves its mouth along its scales, avidly sucking up the droplets. Every now and then it raises its forebody, allowing the water to drain into its stomach. Besides this, the major portion of its fluid requirements are satisfied by its prey, namely the sand-diving lizard (*Aporosaura anchietae*) which has a high moisture content – almost 75% of its body weight.

Little is known about the potency of the venom although, as with the other small adders, it probably causes local necrosis and is unlikely to be fatal.

Peringuey's Adder gives birth to 4-10 young during late February and March. The neonates normally slough their skins within the first hour of life.
☐ **Sandadder, Namib-duinadder.**

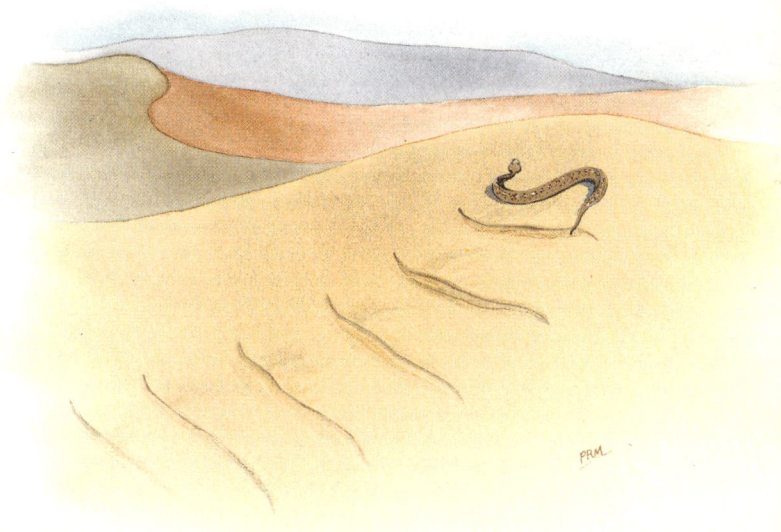

Berg Adder or Cape Mountain Adder
Bitis atropos □ 20-40 cm, exceptionally 60 cm

The head of this species is more elongated than that of most adders but it is still distinct from the neck and relatively slender body. In addition to the coloration illustrated, a drab brownish colour morph occurs in the eastern Transvaal. The Berg Adder has adapted to two diverse habitats: in the central and northern areas of its distribution it occurs in montane grasslands and even above the snowline in the Drakensberg, while in the Cape it is found at sea level.

Mountaineers and rock-climbers who disturb the Berg Adder in its habitat are frequently bitten as it is an irascible species and quick to bite. Unlike most other adders whose venoms are predominantly cytotoxic, the Berg Adder has neurotoxic venom which causes dizziness, drooping eyelids and a temporary loss of the senses of taste and smell. Fortunately most symptoms resolve within a few days and no authenticated fatalities are attributed to this species. Antivenom should not be used.

Diet includes small birds, lizards and rodents with the juveniles showing a preference for frogs.

Females produce up to 15 young in late summer (February/March). Neonates measure 14 cm in length. □ **Bergadder.**

Puff Adder
Bitis arietans arietans
60-100 cm, occasionally longer

Black and yellow Cape colour morph

The most widely distributed venomous snake in Africa. The flat, bluntly spade-shaped head is distinct from the thick body which is covered with keeled scales. Colour varies according to its distribution: generally a drab snake, specimens from Natal and the Cape are frequently strikingly marked in orange or yellow and black. Females have short stubby tails in contrast to the long tapering tails of the males.

Being heavy-bodied and sluggish, the Puff Adder relies on immobility and cryptic camouflage to escape detection. Consequently, animals and humans frequently tread close to or directly on this common snake as it basks in sun-dappled patches along footpaths or in low shrubs. Before striking, the Puff Adder often inflates its body and then exhales rapidly, emitting a loud hissing or puffing sound – hence its common name. The rapid strike and large fangs effectively deliver copious quantities of its potent cytotoxic venom which causes excessive swelling of the bitten limb, followed by severe necrosis and sometimes gangrene. As a result of the massive tissue destruction, a Puff Adder bite is extremely painful and the bitten area takes a long time to heal.

A creature of both diurnal and nocturnal habits, its diet consists mainly of rodents although toads, lizards and birds are also taken. The snake lies in ambush, strikes and then usually releases its victim immediately. The stricken prey continues moving until overcome by the venom: the snake, using its flickering tongue, is able to follow the victim's scent trail. On arriving at the corpse the snake engulfs it without further ado.

Females give birth to 20-50 young in midsummer. ☐ **Pofadder.**

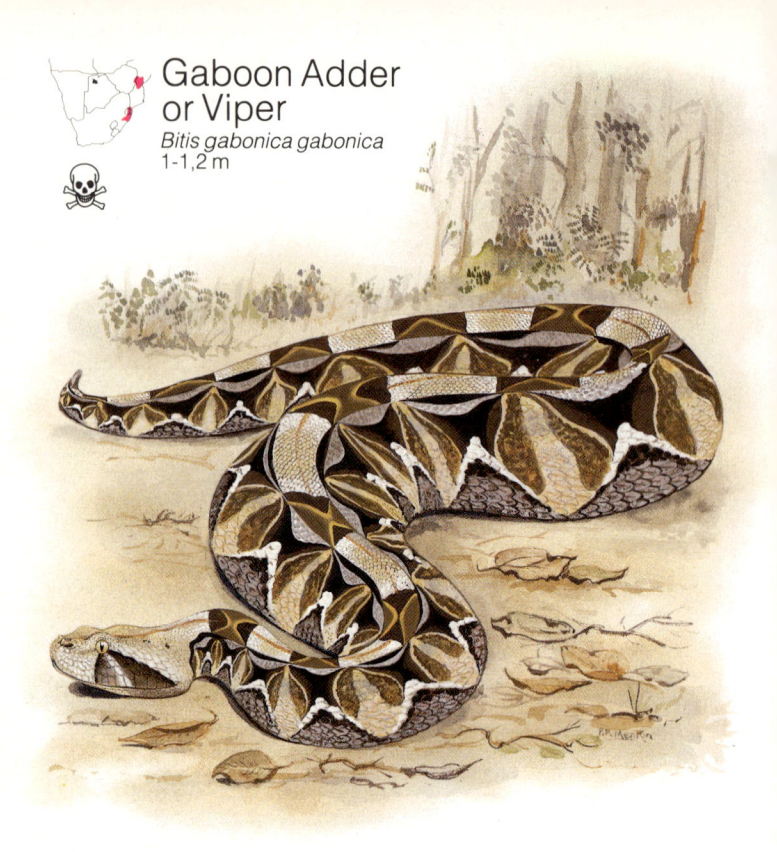

Gaboon Adder or Viper
Bitis gabonica gabonica
1-1,2 m

Restricted to the forested and recently cleared areas of northern Zululand and the lowland forests of eastern Zimbabwe and northern Moçambique, this vivid snake cannot be mistaken for any other. It has a wide, buff-coloured head distinct from a heavy body which is strikingly geometrically patterned in pastel shades that blend perfectly with the leaf litter of the forest floor and make this one of the most effectively camouflaged serpents in Africa.

Its diet consists mainly of rodents but it has been reported as taking birds, mongooses and even monkeys on occasion. After the initial strike, the Gaboon Adder deeply embeds its enormous fangs in its victim. When the animal becomes inactive the snake uses its fangs and teeth to manipulate the prey into a 'head first' position and then slowly swallows it. The Gaboon Adder has the longest fangs (up to 4 cm) of any snake in the world, which enable it to inject massive amounts of its potent cytotoxic venom deep into its victim. Prompt administration of adequate quantities of polyvalent antivenom is necessary to ensure survival.

Broods of 10-13 young are born in late summer. ☐ **Gaboenadder.**

Predation chart

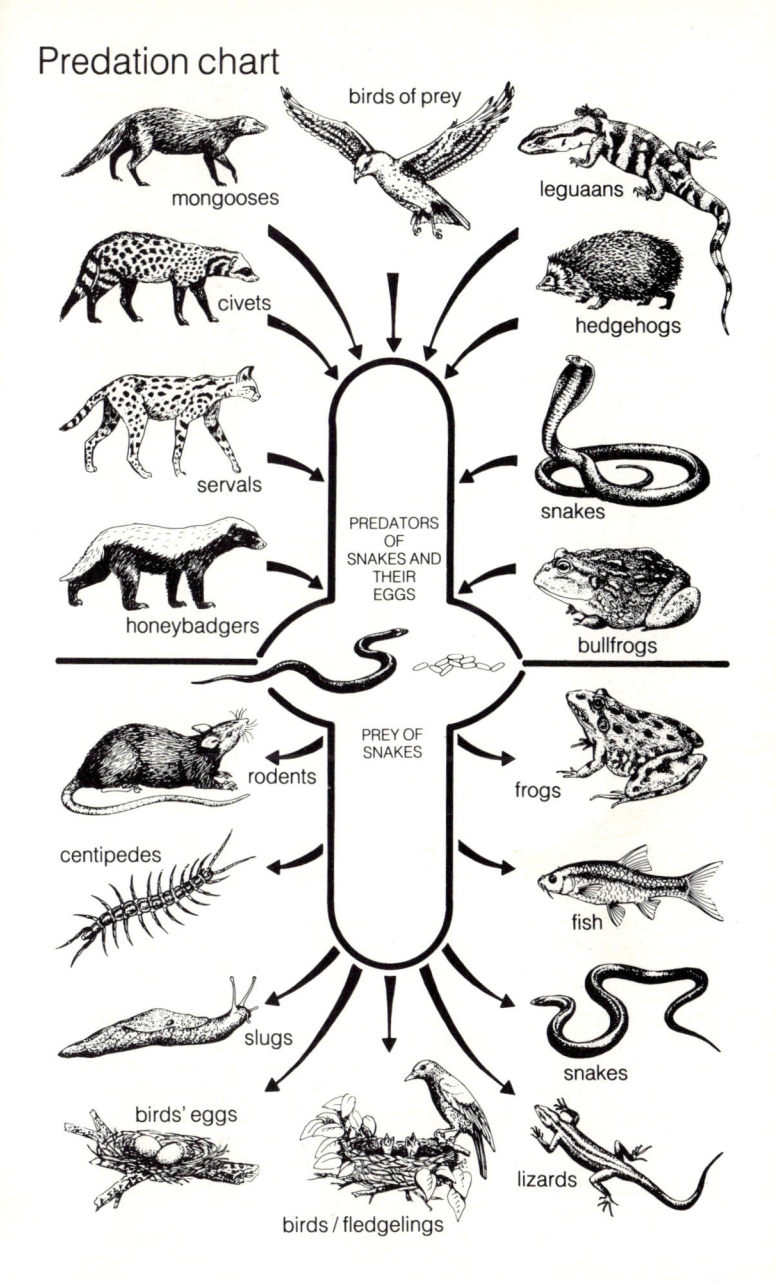

- birds of prey
- mongooses
- leguaans
- civets
- hedgehogs
- servals
- snakes
- honeybadgers
- bullfrogs

PREDATORS OF SNAKES AND THEIR EGGS

PREY OF SNAKES

- rodents
- frogs
- centipedes
- fish
- slugs
- snakes
- birds' eggs
- birds / fledgelings
- lizards

Legislation and conservation

Although South Africa, Namibia and Zimbabwe all have legislation pertaining to reptiles in captivity, most members of the public are totally unaware of these laws. At present the ordinances vary in the extent to which reptiles are 'protected', but in general it is illegal to capture, transport, keep or export a reptile without a permit from the relevant nature conservation body. Besides provincial ordinances, most municipalities have bylaws relating to the caging of wild animals in urban areas. So it is not simply a matter of going out, capturing a snake, placing it in a modified aquarium and bingo! you have an unusual pet. The individual who does this is undoubtedly breaking the law.

The Cape became the first province to protect a species when it passed legislation in the 1950s to save the Mole Snake. Natal followed in 1969 by protecting the Rock Python. Since then, because of the proliferating 'pet' trade, conservation authorities have been including reptiles in their ordinances. Before this time, many reptiles (including snakes) had been collected by schoolboys who sold them to pet shops and snake parks for additional pocket money, and by 'professionals' who collected many hundreds and exported them to the overseas dealers at considerable profit.

Capturing a snake, no matter whether the collector be scientist or amateur, in many instances involves destruction of habitat: termitaria are smashed open, rock slabs are wedged apart, exfoliating bark is pulled off, stones and logs are flipped over. All are situations utilized by reptiles and other vertebrates and invertebrates as retreats, hibernacula and nesting sites, but once destroyed they cannot be used by any of the survivors. The next collector in the area perpetuates the process and within a very short time whole populations can be eradicated.

In addition, southern Africa is a developing area where mining, dam-building, farming, and urban sprawl are ongoing factors. All these result in destruction of snakes' habitats. Veld fires also account for numerous reptilian deaths. Although man, through fear and ignorance, frequently kills snakes when he finds them, certain tribes such as the Bushman – also threatened by 'progress' – rely on them as a food source. Unfortunately the greatest destroyer of snakes is an integral part of the modern world: the tarred road. It is probable that more snakes are killed in one day by vehicles in southern Africa than by all the other causes in a whole year!

In southern Africa only some 16 species are potentially dangerous to man, so by far the majority are innocuous. The diagram on page 49 indicates the snake's role in the food chain. It is not intended to be exhaustive as many other predators and prey exist. We as humans tend to rate other animals according to the benefits we derive from them, but when you next come across a snake, before you are tempted to kill it, consider what use it may be to some other creature in the natural web.

If a snake is killed do not simply discard it: if you cannot identify it, either photograph it or, preferably, take the specimen to a museum, zoo or snake park where it can be identified. Although by no means condoning the killing of snakes, a dead specimen identified (especially if it is a species harmless to man) at least may prevent a repetition of the occurrence.

Locomotion

In snakes, four different kinds of locomotion have been defined: serpentine, rectilinear, side-winding and concertina.

The type of locomotion most frequently used by snakes, particularly the slender, agile forms, is the **serpentine** in which the snake glides forward in a series of waves, much like the propulsive movement of aquatic animals in water. Forward movement is dependent upon the presence of irregularities on the surface over which the snake is moving. Like a horizontal S, the sides of the curves come into contact with rough objects such as grass tufts, pebbles and branches and so propel the body forward. Placed on a highly polished surface the snake slithers but remains in the same place.

Rectilinear locomotion is usual among heavy-bodied species, such as the Puff and Gaboon adders. The snake moves forward in a straight line with no lateral movement: the ventral scales are pulled forward, anchored against a rough surface and then the body is pulled forward over the anchor points. The sequence looks very similar to the movement of a caterpillar.

The **side-winding** and **concertina** modes of progression are specialized and restricted to a few snakes such as Peringuey's Adder and the burrowing forms, *Typhlops* spp., respectively.

Scalation

Considerable variation in scalation exists among the different genera as the texture of the skin and the shape of the scales is an adaptation to the environment of the particular species.
Although some snakes, such as the Shield Snake, have both smooth and keeled scales, most have either one or the other. The type of scale is a diagnostic feature, for example, the cobras are smooth-scaled, the adders keeled-scaled, while 'polished', tightly imbricated scales are typical of the fossorial species.

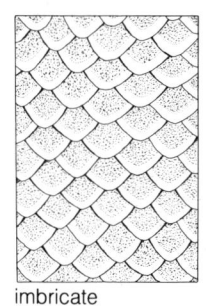

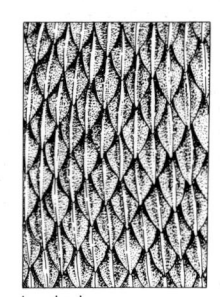

imbricate   smooth   keeled

With the exception of the Blind and Thread snakes where the small scales continue around the body, snakes typically have numerous small scales on the dorsal surface and large transverse scales (which provide traction) on the ventral surface.

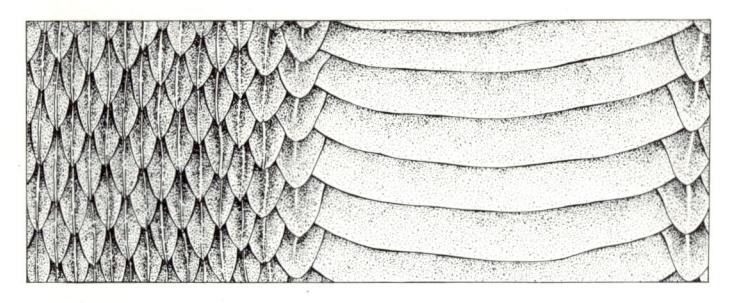

dorsal   ventral

Most snakes shed their skins within the first two weeks of life; some, particularly live-born species, slough within the first hour. Thereafter a snake will shed sporadically throughout its life. Juvenile and sub-adult snakes grow quite rapidly and may shed up to six or seven times a year, whereas adults may shed only once within the same period. There is no seasonal correlation or frequency to this occurrence.

A few days prior to sloughing, the skin becomes lacklustre and the eyes take on an opaque appearance. (Among reptile keepers the snake is said to be 'in the blue'.) At this point the snake is virtually blind and thus tends to be more nervous and irritable. A fluid is secreted between the old external layer of skin and the new, loosening the old layer and allowing it to be shed more easily. The eyes clear and sight is restored. The snake then rubs its snout and forelips against any rough object and the skin peels back off the upper and lower jaws. As the snake slowly moves forward these flaps of skin snag on any abrasive material in the vicinity and the reptile literally crawls out of its old skin, rather like a human removing a sock. A snake slough is usually found inside out.

Dentition

The dentition and cranial structure of snakes is complex and for many years the position of the teeth and/or fangs was the major basis on which snakes were classified. Today classification is dependent on more sophisticated techniques such as research into the snake's genetic make-up as well as the structure and position of various internal organs.

Some snakes such as the Egg-eater are almost devoid of teeth, others such as the Blind Snake have only a few teeth in the upper jaw while the Worm or Thread Snakes possess some teeth only on the bottom jaw.

Snakes use their teeth to grasp prey. In venomous species the fangs, which are modified teeth capable of transporting venom, are used to 'inject' the venom into the prey.

The upper and lower jaws are divided into four longitudinal sections, with the lower jaws separate, loosely connected by ligaments at the front. Snakes usually, but not necessarily always, swallow their prey head first so that fur, feathers or outer skin flows in the correct direction for ease of swallowing. Each 'quarter' of the skull is moved forward alternately over the prey giving the impression that the snake's head is 'walking' over the prey. This disarticulation of the jaw bones, coupled with the production of copious amounts of saliva, enables the snake to engulf animals much larger than its actual head size.

The accompanying illustrations typify the dental structure of the other snakes discussed in this book.

Python skull
The numerous large recurved teeth in both jaws are typical of constrictors. In other fangless (aglyphous) snakes, such as the Brown House-snake, the solid teeth are moderately sized.

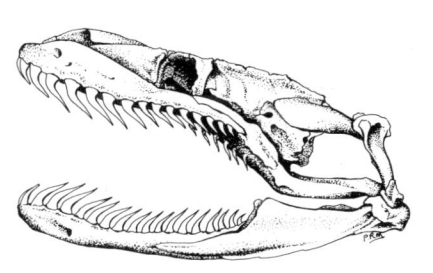

Boomslang skull
Solid teeth in both jaws with one or more grooved fangs below the eye socket on either side of the upper jaw. These rear or back-fanged (opisthoglyphous) snakes comprise nearly half the genera in southern Africa. Only two, namely the Boomslang and the Vine Snake, are dangerous to man.

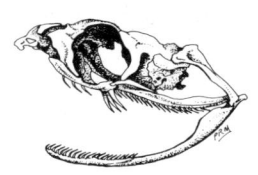

Rinkhals skull
Solid teeth in both jaws with two permanently erect, grooved or hollow fangs at the front of each upper jaw. The front-fanged (proteroglyphous) snakes include the Rinkhals, Cobras, Mambas, Coral Snakes and Sea Snakes.

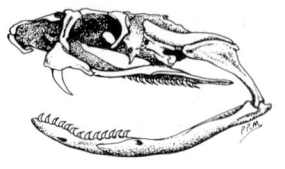

Gaboon Adder skull
Solid teeth in both jaws with two large movable tubular fangs situated at the front of each upper jaw. In southern Africa, those snakes with fangs that fold back along the roof of the mouth when not in use (solenoglyphous snakes) are typified by the Adders.

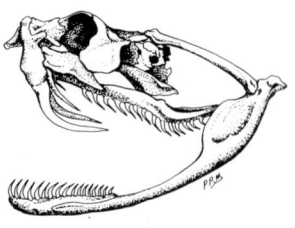

Reproduction

Snakes are not gregarious creatures, tending to be solitary except during hibernation or aestivation when a number, even different species, may congregate in a suitable hibernaculum.

During the mating season, females exude an odour from glands situated near the vent which males detect and follow. Two or three males meeting along this trail may become involved in a ritualistic combat 'dance' where the snakes intertwine and attempt to push each other's neck region to the ground. Mole Snakes actually bite and inflict nasty wounds on each other. The dominant male, on reaching the female, will proceed with jerky, erratic movements to crawl alongside and over her.

Male Black Mambas involved in combat 'dance'.

Male snakes have a pair of copulatory organs (the hemipenes) which are situated behind the vent in the tail, which is why male snakes have larger tails than females. When the vents of both snakes coincide, one of the male's copulatory organs is everted into the cloaca of the female. Copulation itself can be a lengthy process, sometimes lasting a number of hours. Frequently, as has been witnessed in Puff Adders and others, the female will drag the smaller male about as she crawls along. Once copulation is complete the snakes go their separate ways, and no pairing takes place. Females may be fertilized more than once during a mating season by the same and/or other males. Once fertilized, she is capable of retaining viable sperm for a long time, and can produce young for a number of years without further matings.

Puff Adders mating

Some 1-4 months later the egg-laying (oviparous) species will deposit their eggs in a place where there is adequate warmth and humidity, for example, disused termitaria, rock cracks or beneath rotting logs. Pythons and Skaapstekers remain with their eggs during incubation while other species abandon their clutches. Depending on the species and the temperature during this period, hatching occurs between one and seven months later.

The embryo of an oviparous species, when fully developed, has an 'egg tooth' on the tip of its snout, a pin-point projection used to cut a number of slits through the tough, parchment-like skin of the egg. The hatchling then pushes its head through one of the cuts and, as it takes its initial breaths, the remainder of the yolk in the egg is absorbed through the umbilical slit or 'navel'. It crawls out of the egg and, with its yolk reserve (which can sustain it for a number of months), glides off into its new world.

While a clutch is hatching it is extremely vulnerable to predators and, once out of the eggs, the hatchlings disperse in all directions away from the 'nest'.

Live-bearing (viviparous) species produce their young some 3-9 months after fertilization. This method of reproduction has certain advantages over that of the egglayers, inasmuch as the female can ensure fairly constant temperatures (and thus development of embryos) by basking, and the risk of predation is minimized as the gravid female can retire to safe retreats when necessary. At term the female will expel the embryos, each encased in a transparent membranous sac. Jerking and squirming, the neonates break the membranes, rest a while, and then move off as quickly as possible.

Husbandry

Of the many people in southern Africa who keep snakes as pets, most have a genuine interest in their captives, but there are those who attempt to acquire the greatest number of different and dangerous species, possibly to satisfy their ego or to impress others.

It is beyond the scope of this guide to go into detail about husbandry but the following covers the basics.

Having decided that you wish to keep a snake, it is necessary first to obtain a permit from your local Department of Nature Conservation office. The authorities are naturally reluctant to grant permission for people to go out and capture snakes, so you should try to acquire a specimen bred in captivity. An enquiry at your local museum, zoo or reptile park will often gain results: although they may not have specimens available they will frequently know of people who do and whom you can contact.

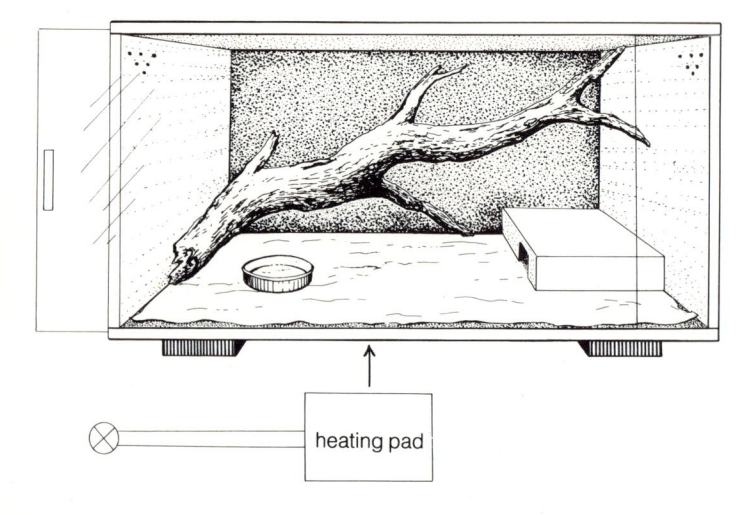

The cage: Aquariums were designed for fish, and should not be used for housing snakes. The all-glass construction and open top lead to innumerable problems. The accompanying illustration gives a good idea of what is required. The cage can be constructed of wood such as marine ply, tempered masonite or even asbestos sheeting. Never use chipboard as it is porous and thus harbours bacteria. All cracks and joints should be sealed before painting the complete unit. To paint, preferably use one of the proprietary brands of polyurethane paint as the resultant hard-wearing finish is well worth the additional expense and effort. The heavy perspex door (or glass, if perspex is not available) should slide open. When closed it must be lockable and have a snug fit all the way around. A few tiny ventilation holes can be drilled in the sides or rear of the cage, but be warned, snakes are the ultimate Houdinis of the animal kingdom! A heating pad, preferably with variable temperature control, should be placed under a portion of the floor of the cage. This will provide a thermal gradient in the cage so that the snake can select the temperature of its choice. Naked light bulbs should not be placed in the cage as a heat source because the snake could burn itself and suffer trauma by being constantly exposed to the light.

Keep the cage furnishings simple. The floor should be covered with newspaper or paper towelling. A water container must be provided; this should be fairly substantial so that the snake is unable to tip it over. A branch can be wedged across the cage and a retreat must be provided. This can be a cardboard box with a suitably sized hole cut in it. A thermometer, preferably a maximum-minimum type (available from most nurseries, or the gardening department at a supermarket), should be installed in the cage.

Probably the most common captive in South Africa is the Brown House-snake — certainly it is the species recommended for the novice snake keeper. A cage 70 cm long, 30 cm wide and 30 cm high would be quite adequate for an adult of this species.

Assuming you have acquired a House-snake, place it in the cage and leave it alone. One of the most common causes of ill-health in captive reptiles is overhandling by their keepers. The only time a captive snake should be handled is during routine cleaning of the cage which may arise at one- to three-week intervals. Observe the new captive: initially it will prowl around and after finding its retreat may remain there for a number of days. Because this is a nocturnal species, its cage should not face a window or a bright light. After a time you will see that the snake emerges in the evening and moves around the cage. Its progress should be unhurried; any frenzied activity indicates an imbalance in the facilities you have provided. Temperatures should be checked daily. A maximum daytime high of 28 °C cooling to a night-time low of 18-20 °C is recommended.

Feeding: Once you are satisfied that the snake has settled into its new environment you can offer it its first meal. House-snakes take rodents so the initial meal should be a small or half-grown mouse (normally available from pet shops), freshly killed and placed in the cage during the evening. It may be necessary to move the mouse around by means of a pair of long forceps to trigger a feeding response. If everything goes according to plan the snake should bite the dead mouse and 'constrict' it. At this point the keeper should back off slowly and allow the snake to swallow its meal with minimal disturbance. Should the snake not take the food immediately leave it in the cage overnight. If it is still not taken, repeat the procedure with another mouse in two or three days' time. Do not become impatient. Remember, a snake just prior to sloughing will not feed, neither will a gravid female nearing the end of her term (the abdominal cavity is filled with eggs or developing embryos so there is no space for food).

The most frequent mistakes made by novice snake-keepers are (a) too much *disturbance*: excessive handling of the snake or movement in the vicinity of the cage; (b) *temperature*: maintaining a snake at constantly low temperatures is a common mistake. A maximum-minimum thermometer is of great value as you can record the highest and lowest temperatures over a 24-hour period. Although daytime temperatures may well be acceptable, often the temperatures at night may be too low and the snake, which depends on warmth to digest its meal, will be reluctant to feed; and (c) *health*: a 'healthy' snake naturally carries a number of bacteria which in themselves cause it no harm, but under adverse conditions such as stress, incorrect temperatures or excessive humidity, the bacterial population explodes and the snake becomes ill. Nasal and oral discharges, gasping, wheezing, loose stools and lethargy are some of the signs of ill-health. The snake should be taken to a vet, zoo or reptile park where the disease can be diagnosed and treatment started.

The Brown House-snake can digest a mouse within 5-14 days and should be allowed to defecate before its next meal. After it has defecated, remove the snake and place it in a holding container. The paper on the floor will have absorbed most of the faeces and can be removed, the cage wiped down with warm water only (certain disinfectants are toxic to snakes) and then refurnished as before, after which the snake can be replaced.

You may have acquired a gravid female or you may be keeping a pair of snakes. If you suspect that the female is going to lay, put her in a separate cage, without a water dish. This is a precautionary measure as females tend to select any moist situation in which to lay and eggs laid in water will 'drown'. Provide her instead with a plastic container (a 5-litre ice-cream tub is ideal for the smaller snakes), cut out an entrance hole and place some moistened paper towelling or moss in it.

Once the eggs have been laid they should be removed for incubation. One of the most popular incubating mediums is vermiculite mixed with water in a 1:1 ratio, that is, 1 g vermiculite to 1 ml water. A plastic tub should be half filled with the medium and the eggs partially submerged. The container should be sealed and placed in a situation where a fairly constant temperature between 25 °C and 28 °C is maintained. During incubation the eggs must not be turned from their original position.

The diet of many hatchlings frequently differs from that of the adults and raising young snakes is a task on its own. To the novice it is suggested that you either release the majority of the clutch in the area from which the parents originated and attempt to raise only one or two specimens, or give them to someone who has experience in raising young snakes.

Snake bite treatment

Only 16 of the 160 species that occur in the area under discussion can be considered potentially dangerous to man. Certain areas, such as the Natal coast and Zululand, have a higher percentage of venomous snakes than others but dangerous snakes occur almost throughout southern Africa. With the increasing interest in outdoor activities in this country, natural areas are being placed under mounting pressure and the risk of snake bite is ever present, albeit of rare occurrence.

In the event of a serious snake bite, adequate quantities of antivenom have to be administered intravenously. Some people are allergic to the antivenom, so the victim should be under medical supervision (preferably in a hospital which has an intensive care unit and where any untoward reactions can be treated promptly). Usually in southern Africa a snake bite victim can be hospitalized within a few hours, therefore it is inadvisable for the first-aider to inject antivenom in the field.

The 'cut and suck' method, along with the use of assorted herbs, gunpowder, Condy's crystals or snake 'stones' belong to a bygone era. Also, a tourniquet applied over-zealously can cause irreparable damage.

In an analysis of 2 538 snake bites which were reported to the South African Institute for Medical Research (where the antivenoms are produced) during the period 1953-1979, Christensen (1981) recorded that 74,4% of the bites were inflicted on the leg, 72,7% being on the lower leg, ankle and foot. The other 'popular' body sites were the hands and arms which accounted for 23,6%, followed by the neck and head (1,3%) and the trunk (0,7%). The above statistics are important because the first-aid procedure described below can be used in the majority of cases.

Snake bite first aid (After Sutherland, 1985)

Whenever you go on an outdoor excursion be sure to take three or four 100 mm wide crêpe bandages. Should a snake bite occur on the foot or leg, 1) immediately apply the crêpe bandage over the bite and 2) continue to wind it up the limb until you reach the groin. Two or three bandages may be necessary and you should apply them as tightly as you would for a sprained ankle. Keep the bitten limb as still as possible during this procedure. Do not remove clothing, merely roll the bandage over it. 3) Afterwards, using a further bandage, strap a splint to the limb to immobilize it. It is believed that venom is dispersed via the lymph glands and the application of a broad crêpe bandage over the bite and up the bitten limb inhibits the spread of the venom.

The same procedure should be followed for a bite on the hand or arm. Apply the bandages from hand to armpit, splint from hand to elbow, then place the arm in a sling. In both instances the bandages can be left in place for a number of hours.

In the case of a bite on the trunk, neck or head, apply firm pressure to the bitten area if possible.

Carry the victim to the nearest vehicle or better still, if it is practical, bring the vehicle to the victim. If the victim has to walk, he should do so calmly and slowly. Get the victim to hospital as soon as possible.

If the snake can be killed without endangering anyone's life, then do so. Carry the snake *by the tail* to the hospital, where it can be identified.

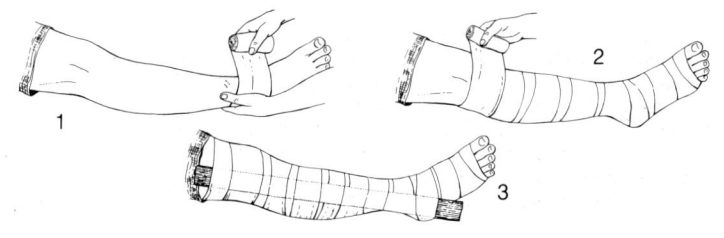

Spitting snakes

Venom in the eyes causes intense smarting and the eyes and nose weep copiously. **Do not rub** the eyes, and if a small child or pet is the victim, prevent it from doing so. Holding the eyelids open, flush the eyes with any bland fluid that is readily available. There is a popular misconception that milk is beneficial, but certainly it is no more so than any other bland fluid. Generally water is the easiest to obtain but in a desperate situation cold drink, tea, beer or even urine could be used. Venom in the eyes is not life-threatening but could cause partial blindness; in any event a doctor should be consulted as soon as possible.

Antivenoms

Two antivenoms are produced by the South African Institute for Medical Research (SAIMR) for use in southern Africa: monovalent Boomslang antivenom which is specifically for use against that snake's venom, and polyvalent antivenom which is effective against the venom of the Black and Green Mambas, the Rinkhals, the Cobras as well as the Puff and Gaboon Adders. Because the venoms of the less toxic species such as the Horned and Berg Adders, the Shield Snake and Coral Snake, are not used in the production of the polyvalent antivenom, it is not effective against the bites of these snakes. Envenomation by these species is treated symptomatically.

The most effective route of administering antivenom is by intravenous injection. As antivenom is a 'foreign' protein, there is the risk of a severe, possibly life-threatening reaction when it is injected and it should thus only be administered under medical supervision and at a hospital geared for such an emergency.

Glossary

Terms used in this book as they pertain to snakes.

Aestivation: Dormancy during summer or the dry season.
Aglyph: A snake in which no tooth has a groove or canal; by inference a snake which has no fangs.
Arboreal: Living in trees.
Cloaca: A cavity in the pelvic region into which the alimentary canal and the genital and urinary ducts open.
Crepuscular: Active at dusk.
Cytotoxic: Adversely affecting tissue and cell formation.
Diurnal: Active during the day.
Dorsal: The side of the snake which is normally directed upwards with reference to gravity.
Ectotherm: An organism that regulates the body temperature chiefly by means of external sources of heat.
Endemic: Confined to a given region.
Fossorial: Living below ground.

Gangrene: Death and decay of body tissue.
Gravid: Pregnant. In reptiles, carrying young or eggs.
Haemotoxin: A venom component which adversely affects the blood or the circulatory system.
Hatchling: A new-born snake produced by an egg-laying (oviparous) species. *See also* Neonate.
Hibernaculum: Place used by reptiles during winter dormancy.
Imbricate: Overlapping, as the shingles on a roof.
Interstitial: Intervening area of skin between individual scales.
Keel: The slight ridge on the upper surface of each scale, present in some species.
Morph: A specific type, variety or form.
Myotoxin: Toxin present in venom which acts on muscle tissue.
Necrosis: Death of tissue or organ.
Neonate: A new-born snake produced by live-bearing (viviparous) species. *See also* Hatchling.
Neurotoxin: Toxin present in snake venom which acts on nerve tissue.
Nocturnal: Active at night.
Obtuse: Of blunt shape, not sharp or pointed.
Opisthoglyph: A venomous snake with the fangs in the posterior part of the mouth; a rear or 'back-fanged' snake.
Oviparous: Producing young from eggs which are expelled from the body and where the embryonic development takes place outside the female.
Proteroglyph: A snake with fangs mounted on a relatively fixed and immovable bone in the front of the mouth.
Race: A group sharing common characteristics that distinguish them from other members of the same species, usually forming a geographically isolated group.
Recurved (teeth): Projecting rearwards. In snakes, the tips of the teeth point towards the throat.
Rostral: The scale at the tip of the snout.
Solenoglyph: A snake with fangs mounted on a rotatable maxillary bone, so that the fang can be folded flat against the roof of the mouth.
Terrestrial: Living on the ground.
Vent: The external opening of the urinary and genital system.
Ventral: The side of the snake which is normally directed downwards with reference to gravity.
Viviparous: Having embryos which develop within the mother.

Suggested further reading

The following list will assist those interested in gaining more detailed information about snakes and their habits.

General
Bellairs, A. 1969. *The Life of Reptiles*. Vols. 1 & 2. Weidenfeld & Nicolson, London.
Broadley, D. G. 1983. *FitzSimons' Snakes of Southern Africa*. Rev. ed. Delta Books, Johannesburg.

Broadley, D. G. and Cock, E. V. 1975. *Snakes of Rhodesia*. Bundu Series. Longman, Rhodesia.

FitzSimons, V. F. M. 1962. *The Snakes of Southern Africa*. Purnell & Sons, Cape Town.

FitzSimons, V. F. M. 1974. *A Field Guide to the Snakes of Southern Africa*. 2nd ed. Collins, London.

Jacobsen, N. H. G. and Haacke, W. D. 1980. *Harmless Snakes of the Transvaal*. Transvaal Nature Conservation Division Information Series 2.

Marais, J. J. 1985. *Snake versus Man*. Macmillan, Johannesburg.

Peters, J. A. 1964. *Dictionary of Herpetology*. Hafner, New York.

Pienaar, U. de V., Haacke, W. D. and Jacobsen, N. H. G. 1983. *The Reptiles of the Kruger National Park*. National Parks Board, Pretoria.

Rose, W. 1962. *The Reptiles and Amphibians of Southern Africa*. Rev. ed. Maskew Miller, Cape Town.

Visser, J. 1979. *Common Snakes of South Africa*. Purnell, Cape Town.

Husbandry

Cooper, J. E. and Jackson, O. F., eds. 1981. *Diseases of the Reptilia*. Vols. 1 & 2. Academic Press, London.

Frye, F. L. 1981. *Biomedical and Surgical Aspects of Captive Reptile Husbandry*. V. M. Publishing, Edwardsville.

Lucas, J., ed. 1969. *International Zoo Yearbook*. Vol. 9. Zool. Soc. of London, London.

Mattison, C. 1982. *The Care of Reptiles and Amphibians in Captivity*. Blandford Press, Dorset.

Olney, P. J. S., ed. 1979. *International Zoo Yearbook*. Vol. 19. Zool. Soc. of London, London.

Snake bite

Branch, W. R. (n.d.) *First Aid Treatment of Snakebite*. Port Elizabeth Museum.

Branch, W. R. 1985. *The Pressure/Immobilisation First Aid Treatment of Snakebite*. J. Herp. Assoc. Afr. 31, pp. 10-13.

Christensen, P. A. 1981. *Snakebite and the Use of Antivenom in Southern Africa*. S. Afr. Med. J. 59, pp. 934-938.

Patterson, R. W. (n.d.) *Treatment of Snake Bite*. Transvaal Snake Park.

Reitz, C. J. 1978. *Poisonous South African Snakes and Snakebite*. Perskor, Pretoria.

Sutherland, S. K. 1985. *First Aid for Snakebite*. Litt. Serp. 5(2). pp. 71-75.

Tilbury, C. R. 1982. *Observations on the bite of the Mozambique Spitting Cobra (Naja m. mossambica)*. S. Afr. Med. J. 61, pp. 308-313.

Visser, J. 1982. *Dangerously Venomous Snakes and the Effects and Treatment of Snakebite*. Camps Bay.

Visser, J. and Chapman, D. S. 1978. *Snakes and Snakebite*. Purnell, Cape Town.

INDEX

Numbers in **bold type** indicate the main species entry.

A
Adder 54
  Berg **46**, 60
  Berg- **46**
  Cape Mountain **46**
  Gaboen- **48**
  Gaboon **48**, 51, 54, 60
  Horing- **42**
  Horned **42**, 43, 60
  Many-horned, Western **43**
  Peringuey's Desert 42, **44**, 51
  Pof- **47**
  Puff **36**, **47**, 51, 55, 60
  Sand- **45**
  Side-winding **44**
  Veelhoring- **43**
Amplorhinus multimaculatus **14**
Aparallactus capensis **17**
Aspidelaps lubricus infuscatus 31
  l. lubricus **31**
Aspidelaps scutatus scutatus **32**
Atractaspis bibronii **22**
Aurora Snake **8**, 21

B
Beaked Snake, Rufous **15**
Bird Snake **27**
Bitis arietans arietans **47**
  atropos **46**
  caudalis **42**
  cornuta cornuta **43**
  c. inornata 43
  gabonica gabonica **48**
  peringueyi **44**
Black-headed Snake 10, **17**, 22
Blind Snake 21, 22, 53
  Bibron's **4**, 5
  Schlegel's **5**
Boomslang 23, **26**, 28, 53
Bosslang, Gespikkelde **23**
Bush Snake **22**
  Spotted **23**

C
Causus defilippii **41**
  rhombeatus **41**
Centipede-eater, Cape **17**
Cobra, 11, 54, 60
  Banded **32**
  Bushveld **32**
  Cape **34**, 35
  Egyptian **32**
  Forest **35**
  King **38**
  Spitting, Black **36**
  Spitting, Moçambique **36**
  Spitting, Western Barred **36**
Coral Snake **31**, 54, 60
Coral Snake, Western 31
Crotaphopeltis hotamboeia **24**

D
Dasypeltis scabra **13**
Dendroaspis angusticeps **39**
  polylepis **38**
Dispholidus typus typus **26**
Duberria lutrix lutrix **10**
Duinadder, Namib- **45**

E
Egg-eater, Common 10, **13**, 53
Eiervreter, Gewone **14**
Elapsoidea spp. **29**
Erdslang, Bibron se **5**
  Reuse **5**
Erdslangetjie, Glansende **6**

F
File Snake, Cape **11**

G
Garter Snakes **29**
Geelslang, Kaapse **34**
Graafneusslang **20**
Grass Snakes **18**
  Cross-marked **19**
  Olive **18**
Green Snake, South-eastern 22, 23
Grondslang, Spitsneus- **18**

H
Haakneusslang **15**
Harlequin Snake, Spotted **20**, 21
  Striped **9**, 21
Hemachatus haemachatus **30**
Herald Snake **24**, 25
Homoroselaps dorsalis **21**
  lacteus **20**
Horingsmannetjie **42**, **43**
House-snake **10**
  Brown **9**, 11, 53, 57, 58
Huisslang, Bruin **9**

I
imFezi **36**

K
Kapel, Bosveld **33**
Kobra, Bontlip- **35**
  Bos- **35**
  Egiptiese **33**
  Kaapse **34**
Koraalslang **31**
Kousbandjie **21**
Kousbandslang **29**
Kousbandslangetjie **21**

L
Lamprophis aurora **8**
  fuliginosus **9**
Leptotyphlops scutifrons scutifrons **6**
Luislang, Gewone **7**
Lycodonomorphus rufulus **7**
Lycophidion capense capense **10**

M
Mamba 54
  Black **38**, 39, 60
  Green 22, **39**, 60
  Groen **39**
  Swart **39**
Many-spotted Snake, Cape **14**
Mehelya capensis capensis **11**
Mierslang, Swartkop- **17**
Mole Snake 11, **12**, 50, 54
Molslang **13**

N
Nagadder **41**
  Wipneus **41**
Nagslang, Aurora **9**
Naja haje annulifera **32**
  melanoleuca **35**
  mossambica **36**
  nigricollis nigricincta **36**
  n. woodi 36
  nivea **34**
Night-adder, Common 13, **41**
  Snouted 38, **41**

O
Ophiophagus hannah **38**

P
Pelamis platurus **40**
Philothamnus hoplogaster **22**
  semivariegatus semivariegatus **23**
Prosymna sundevallii sundevallii **20**
Psammophis crucifer **19**
  leightoni trinasalis **19**
  phillipsii **18**
  sibilans brevirostris **18**
  subtaeniatus subtaeniatus **18**

Psammophylax rhombeatus
  rhombeatus 16
  tritaeniatus 16
Pseudaspis cana 12
Python 53, 55
  Rock 6, 50
Python sebae natalensis 6
Python, Southern African 6

Q
Quill-snouted Snake, Striped 17

R
Red-lipped Snake 24
Reed Snake, Cape 14
Rhamphiophis oxyrhynchus rostratus 15
Rietslang, Kaapse 15
Rinkhals 30, 54, 60
Rooilipslang 25

S
Sandslange 19
Sand Snake, Forked-marked 19
  Short-snouted 18
  Stripe-bellied 18
  Yellow-bellied 18
Sea Snake 54
  Yellow-bellied 40

Sebraslang 36
Seeslang, Swart-en-geel 40
Shield Snake 32, 51, 60
Shield-nose Snake 32
Shovel-snout, Southern 20
  Sundevall's 20
Skaapsteker 16, 55
  Gestreepte 16
  Spotted 16
  Striped 16
Skildneusslang 32
Slakvreter, Gewone 11
Slug-eater, Common 10
Spoegkobra, Mosambiek 37
Stiletto Snake, Bibron's 22
  Southern 22
Sweepslange 19
Sypikslang 22

T
Telescopus beetzii 25
  semiannulatus polystictus 25
  s. semiannulatus 25
Thelotornis capensis capensis 27
  c. mossambicanus 27
  c. oatesii 27
Thread Snake, Peters' 6, 53
Tierslang, Gewone 25
Tiger Snake, Eastern 25

Tree Snake 26
Twig Snake 27
Typhlops bibronii 4
  schlegelii subspp. 5, 51

V
Vine Snake 27, 53
Viper, Gaboon 48
Voëlslang 28
Vylslang, Kaapse 11

W
Waterslang, Bruin 8
Waterslang, Gewone Groen 23
Water-snake 11
  Brown 7
  Green 22
Wolfslang, Kaapse 10
Wolf Snake, Cape 10, 22
Worm Snake 21, 53
  Peters' 6

X
Xenocalamus bicolor lineatus 17

Struik Publishers (Pty) Ltd
(a member of Struik New Holland Publishing (Pty) Ltd)
Cornelis Struik House
80 McKenzie Street
Cape Town 8001

Reg. No.: 54/00965/07

First published in hardcover 1986
First published in softcover 1989
Second softcover edition 1993

10 9 8 7 6 5 4 3 2

Copyright © text and maps: R.W. Patterson
Copyright © illustrations: P.R. Meakin
Copyright © in published edition Struik New Holland Publishing (Pty) Ltd 1986, 1989, 1993

Set by McManus Bros (Pty) Ltd, Cape Town
Reproduction by Unifoto (Pty) Ltd, Cape Town
Printed and bound by CTP Book Printers (Pty) Ltd

All rights reserved. No part of this publication may be reproduced, stored
in a retrieval system, or transmitted, in any form or by any means, electronic,
mechanical, photocopying, recording or otherwise, without the prior written
permission of the copyright owners and publishers.

ISBN 1 86825 428 3